PIGS

BY CYNTHIA AMOROSO AND BOB NOYED

PUBLISHED BY THE CHILD'S WORLD®

The Child's World®
childsworld.com

Published by The Child's World®
1980 Lookout Drive • Mankato, MN 56003-1705
800-599-READ • www.childsworld.com

ACKNOWLEDGMENTS
The Child's World®: Mary Swensen, Publishing Director
The Design Lab: Design
Michael Miller: Editing
Sarah M. Miller: Editing

DESIGN ELEMENTS
© Doremi/Shutterstock.com

PHOTO CREDITS
© Baloncici/Bigstockphoto.com: 14-15; Dusan Petkovic/
Shutterstock.com: 10; dyoma/Shutterstock.com: 12;
Luisa Leal Photography/Shutterstock.com: 18; Nut Iamsupasit/
Shutterstock.com: cover; Perfect Lazybones/Bigstockphoto.com:
20-21; Rade Hadzic/Shutterstock.com: 13; Sarah Hart Morgan/
Shutterstock.com: 8-9; TippaPatt/Shutterstock.com: 16; Tsekhmister/
Bigstockphoto.com: 6; yobro/Bigstockphoto.com: 19; Yulia
Grigoryeva/Shutterstock.com: 5

ISBN: 9781503808294
LCCN: 2015958462

Printed in the United States of America
Mankato, MN
June, 2016
PA02308

Table of Contents

Oink, Snort, Squeal...4

Thick Bodies...7

Round Snouts...11

Males and Females...12

Baby Pigs...14

Eating...17

Important Pigs...18

Glossary...22

To Learn More...23

Index...24

About the Authors...24

Oink, Snort, Squeal

"Oink!" "Snort!" "Squeal!" What animals make these sounds? Pigs make these sounds!

DID YOU KNOW?

MOST FARM PIGS WEIGH BETWEEN 110 AND 770 POUNDS (50 AND 350 KILOGRAMS).

DID YOU KNOW?
A GROUP OF PIGS IS CALLED A HERD.

Thick Bodies

Pigs have thick bodies. They have four short legs and a curly tail. Pigs have four toes. They walk on their tiptoes.

Pigs can be many colors. Some are pink or brown. Others are black and white. Pigs are covered with coarse hair.

DID YOU KNOW?

PIGS CANNOT SWEAT. THEY OFTEN ROLL IN MUD TO KEEP COOL.

9

DID YOU KNOW?

PIGS CAN EVEN SMELL THINGS THAT ARE UNDERGROUND.

Round Snouts

Pigs have a round nose called a **snout**. They use it to smell and feel around. Pigs have a great sense of smell!

Males and Females

A male pig is called a **boar**.

A female pig is called a **sow**.

Baby Pigs

Baby pigs are called **piglets**. A sow can have eight to twelve piglets at a time. Piglets drink their mother's milk.

DID YOU KNOW?
NEWBORN PIGLETS WEIGH ABOUT 2.5 POUNDS (A LITTLE MORE THAN 1 KILOGRAM).

16

Eating

Farm pigs eat corn, oats, and other grains. Pigs will eat almost anything!

Important Pigs

Most pigs are raised for meat.
This meat is called **pork**.

Pigs are also raised for their skin. It is made into **leather**. Footballs, belts, and gloves are made from pigskin.

Pigs are smart animals. They can learn tricks. Some people have pigs as pets. Would you like a pig as a pet?

DID YOU KNOW?

POT-BELLIED PIGS ARE OFTEN KEPT AS PETS.

Glossary

BOAR (BOR) A boar is a male pig.

LEATHER (LETH-ur) Leather is the skin of animals that has been treated and dried. Pigskins are used to make leather.

PIGLETS (PIG-lets) Piglets are baby pigs.

PORK (PORK) Pork is the meat from pigs.

SNOUT (SNOWT) A pig's nose is its snout.

SOW (SOW) A sow is a female pig.

To Learn More

IN THE LIBRARY

Macken, JoAnn Early. *Pigs*. Pleasantville, NY: Weekly Reader Publishing, 2010.

Minden, Cecilia. *Farm Animals: Pigs*. Ann Arbor, MI: Cherry Lake Publishing, 2010.

Nelson, Robin. *Pigs*. Minneapolis, MN: Lerner, 2009.

ON THE WEB

Visit our Web site for links about pigs:
childsworld.com/links

Note to Parents, Teachers, and Librarians: We routinely verify our Web links to make sure they are safe and active sites. So encourage your readers to check them out!

Index

appearance, 7, 8, 11
as pets, 20

boar, 12

colors, 8

eating, 14, 16, 17

hair, 8
herd, 6

importance, 18, 19

leather, 19
legs, 7

piglets, 14, 15
pork, 18
pot-bellied pigs, 20

rolling in mud, 9

sense of smell, 10, 11
size, 5, 7
smart, 20
snout, 11

sounds, 4
sow, 13, 14
sweating, 9

tail, 7
teeth, 12
toes, 7

weight, 5, 15

ABOUT THE AUTHORS

Cynthia Amoroso is an assistant superintendent in a Minnesota school district. She enjoys reading, writing, gardening, traveling, and spending time with friends and family.

Bob Noyed has worked in school communications and public relations. He continues to write for both children and adult audiences. Bob lives in Woodbury, Minnesota.